I Get the Feeling That **Nobukuni**-san **Likes Me**

1

Story & Art by
KOSUKE YASUDA

CONTENTS

I'M HOME!

TMP TMP TMP TMP TMP TMP

WEL-COME BACK!

WHERE'S THAT GIRL *BEEN* ALL DAY?

I HAD THE DAY OFF, BUT SHE SAID SOMETHING ABOUT GOING INTO TOWN.

WELL, SHE *IS* AROUND THAT AGE. MAYBE SHE WENT ON A DATE.

Period 1 | Charm Guys with Armpit Pheromones?!

KNOCK IT OFF! BOYS AND DATING ARE BEYOND HER!
Giggle Giggle
RUSTLE
SO TRUE ...
HER TOTAL LACK OF INTEREST IS ALMOST WORRYING.
I'M SURE SHE WAS OFF BUYING ONE OF THOSE NOVELS SHE LOVES SO MUCH.
I WONDER WHAT SERIOUS BOOK...
JKteen
SHE BOUGHT THIS TIME?
FWIP FWIP FWIP
TA-DA!!
Leading Lost Lambs to Love
Meeko, the Relationship Guru's Advice for your Love Life
THERE'S A NEW ARTICLE THIS WEEK!
JKteen
FROM MEEKO, THE RELATIONSHIP GURU!

THE GIRL I WAS UNTIL NOW...
HAD NO INTEREST IN TEEN FASHION MAGAZINES.
I ONLY CARED ABOUT BOOKS, ESPECIALLY THE ONES I LOVED GROWING UP.
BUT I'M DIFFERENT NOW. WELL, IT'S MORE LIKE I NEED TO CHANGE THE WAY I AM.
TO HAVE ANY CHANCE...
OF FALLING IN LOVE!
UH-HUH, I SEE... GOTTA REMEMBER THIS FOR LATER!

SORRY, NOBU-KUNI-SAN.
SINCE WE SIT NEXT TO EACH OTHER, YOU'RE ALWAYS STUCK SHARING YOUR TEXTBOOK WITH ME.
IT'S NOT A PROBLEM! BESIDES, YOU JUST TRANS-FERRED HERE.
UNTIL YOUR BOOKS ARRIVE, YOU DON'T HAVE A CHOICE.

THOUGH I WOULDN'T MIND IF THEY NEVER ARRIVE...
わか
HAPPY
ほん
HAPPY
ほわ
FUZZ
WARM
ほわ
GASP!
THIS IS NO TIME TO BASK IN THE GLOW OF HAPPINESS!
I CAN'T LET THIS CHANCE GO TO WASTE!
I GOTTA PUT MEEKO-SAMA'S ADVICE TO THE TEST...
SO SASAKI-KUN WILL FALL IN LOVE WITH ME!
...?

CHECK!
Charm Guys with Armpit Pheromones!?
Armpit...
Pher...
GRIP
Phero-mones...?
WOBBLE
I DON'T GET IT. HOW EXACTLY DO I GET THE PHEROMONES TO COME OUT OF MY ARMPITS? MAYBE IF I MOVE MY ARM LIKE THIS...
WOW, THIS IS HARDER THAN I THOUGHT. (TALKING TO HERSELF.)
AM I DOING THIS RIGHT?!
WHAM!!
OW.
OOPS!

SORRY.
SHF...
HUH? WAIT, NO! IT'S MY FAU--
AAAH!
I'M SO SORRY ...
HUH?! I DON'T GET IT! I DID EXACTLY WHAT MEEKO-SAMA TOLD ME TO!
I MUST BE DOING SOMETHING WRONG...
BLUSH BLUSH
WHAT DO I DO NOW ...?
OH! MAYBE I NEED TO EXPOSE MY ARMPIT?
LET'S GIVE IT A SHOT.
PULL
FIDGET FIDGET

ARE THE PHEROMONES COMING OUT YET?
ぐにぐに
SQUISH SQUISH

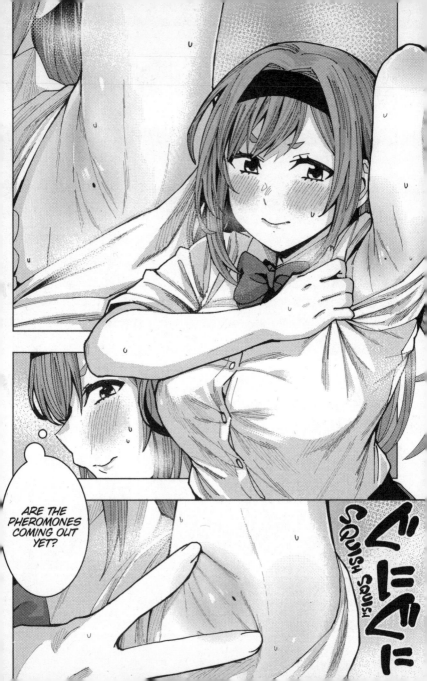

FWIP

WHY DID HE TURN AWAY?

Oh no!

...?

?

...!

NO NO NO...

NOoo!

NO NO NO...

I SMELL?!

DON'T TELL ME...

11

Eeeek!
COME TO THINK OF IT, I SPENT ALL OF LAST WEEKEND COOPED UP IN MY ROOM, AND MOM SAID...
For the love of God, open a window!
It reeks in here...
Of **me**?!
I RUN HOT, SO I TEND TO SWEAT EASILY...
AND IT'S THE AFTERNOON, WHICH MEANS I'M A STINK MACHINE...
HE'S GONNA THINK I'M A SMELLY FREAK AT THIS RATE...
BUT MEEKO-SAMA DID SAY...
THAT PHEROMONES ARE MIXED IN WITH ARMPIT AROMA.
SO THE SMELLIER THE ARMPIT, THE STRONGER THE PHEROMONES...
IF THE POWER OF MY PHEROMONES CANCELS OUT MY NATURAL BODY ODOR...
THEN MAYBE I'LL BREAK EVEN... AND THEN HE MIGHT ACTUALLY...
...?!
びくっ
FLINCH!

DON'T HATE ME...
PLEASE DON'T HATE ME FOR EXPOSING MY ARM-PITS...
YOU ADDED ANOTHER ARMPIT WHILE I WASN'T LOOKING...
.....
UH, NOBU-KUNI-SAN?
ARE YOU OKAY?
TOTALLY...
THERE'S A LOT I DON'T GET ABOUT GIRLS...
BUT I FEEL LIKE YOU PROBABLY SHOULDN'T BE WAVING YOUR ARMS AROUND LIKE THAT IN FRONT OF A BUNCH OF GUYS.
HOW DO I PUT THIS...
※ He thinks this is a secret girl ritual boys don't understand.
I CAN SEE YOUR BRA... AND OTHER STUFF YOU PROBABLY DON'T WANT ME TO SEE...
!!!

I'M S-S-SOOO SORRY!
I GAVE YOU AN UNINTENTIONAL EYEFUL ALONG WITH BEING SMELLY.
HUH? WAIT, WHAT? SMELLY?
I'M SORRY... STARTING TOMORROW, I'LL USE A BOTTLE OF FEBREEZE BEFORE SCHOOL...
YOU SMELL FINE TO ME.
I JUST WANTED TO GIVE YOU A HEADS UP. I'M SURE YOU DON'T WANT TO ACCIDENTALLY FLASH EVERYONE ...
I...
I DOUBT ANYONE WOULD ENJOY SEEING MY BODY, SO IT'S NO BIG DEAL...
THAT'S NOT TRUE.
HUH?
I... DON'T AGREE WITH YOUR OPINION.

EEEEEE!

EEEEE
...

OH, MEEKO-SAMA...

SIGH...

I MESSED UP BIG TIME...
I APPRECIATE YOUR ADVICE, BUT I COULDN'T MAKE IT WORK...
...
She won a Meeko plushie as a longtime reader.
BUT I KNOW THAT SOME-DAY...
SASAKI-KUN WILL NOTICE ME!
I'M A PLAIN COUNTRY GIRL WHO'S CLUELESS ...
AND NOW I'M A HIGH SCHOOLER WITH ZERO RELATIONSHIP EXPERIENCE.
BUT I HAVE YOUR WEEKLY COLUMN TO LEAD ME IN THE RIGHT DIRECTION!
IF I READ IT EVERY WEEK, THEN EVEN SOMEONE LIKE ME COULD FIND LOVE...
......
......
YOU BETTER NOT BE STRINGING ME ALONG.
AND THUS, NOBUKUNI NODOKA FAITHFULLY FOLLOWS MEEKO-SAMA'S LOVE LESSONS, ONE WEEK AFTER ANOTHER.

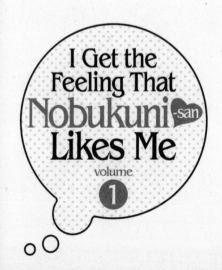

I Get the
Feeling That
Nobukuni-san
Likes Me

volume
1

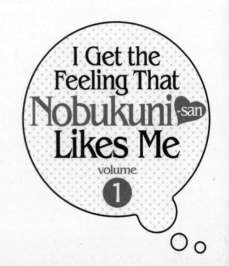

I Get the
Feeling That
Nobukuni-san
Likes Me

volume
1

Period 2   The Allure of a Sleeping Beauty?!

Whisp
NOBU-KUNI-SAN...
GASP!
はっ
ARE YOU OKAY?
Y-YEAH ...
THANKS ...
I WAS READING A BOOK LAST NIGHT AND STAYED UP WAY TOO LATE...
MY EYE-LIDS FEEL ...
WOBBLE
SO ...
HEAVY ...
DROOP
ゴン
THUNK
ZZZ すう
...
SHE FELL ASLEEP ...
すう ZZZ
CUTE...
?!

かぁあああっ
BLUUUUUUUSH
......
......
ARE YOU AWAKE, NOBUKUNI-SAN?
EEP!
SNORE
SNORRRE
MUST BE MY IMAGINATION.
SHE LOOKS SO TIRED... I'D FEEL BAD WAKING HER UP. GUESS IT'S OKAY AS LONG AS THE TEACHER DOESN'T NOTICE.
PH...

PHEW! THAT WAS CLOSE...
WITH MEEKO-SAMA'S ADVICE...
SASAKI-KUN IS AS GOOD AS MINE!!
CHECK!
The Allure of a Sleeping Beauty?!
Sleeping beauty?
THERE'S NO WAY I'D LET MYSELF ACTUALLY FALL ASLEEP IN FRONT OF HIM, WITH MY EYELIDS HALF SHUT AND MOUTH WIDE OPEN...
BUT WHAT IF I WERE TO PRETEND TO BE ASLEEP...
IF I STAY IN THIS POSITION, HE WON'T BE ABLE TO SEE MY FACE AND I'LL FALL ASLEEP FOR REAL...
MM~...
SNAG
?!
HUH? I THINK ONE OF THE BUTTONS ON MY SHIRT IS CAUGHT ON MY TEXTBOOK...
WHAT IN THE... HUH?
PULL
UGH...!!
COME ON!
YANK

SNAP
!!
?!!

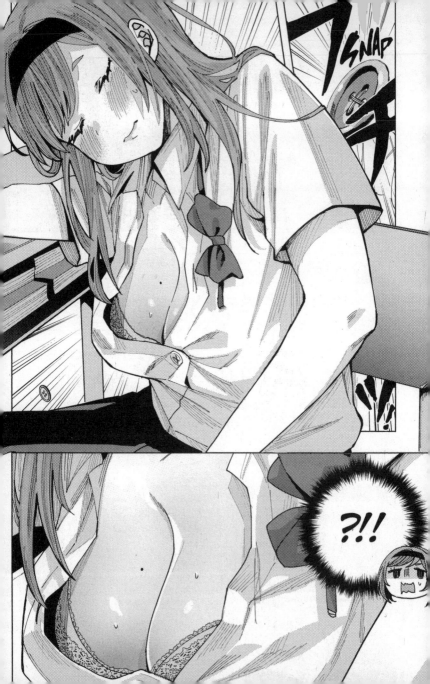

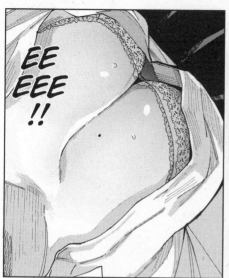

WH- WHAT JUST HAPPENED? I THINK I MANAGED TO RIP MY SHIRT WIDE OPEN!!
AND I'M GIVING EVERYONE A FREE SHOW!!
PEEK
HOW BAD IS IT...?
EE EEE !!
WHAT DID I DO TO DESERVE THIS?! IF I DON'T COVER UP, THE CLASS CREEPS MIGHT GET THE WRONG IDEA...
WAIT, NO... I'M SUPPOSED TO BE ASLEEP. IF I START FLAILING AROUND, I'LL BLOW MY COVER...
CHECK!
The
a Sleeping Beauty!
MEEKO-SAMA SAID BOYS LIKE IT WHEN GIRLS FALL ASLEEP NEAR THEM...
THEY FIND THAT VULNERABILITY ADORABLE...
THERE'S NO ONE MORE VULNERABLE THAN ME RIGHT NOW (IT'S TRUE).
THIS IS MY CHANCE TO GROW AS A WOMAN!!
IF NOTHING ELSE, I'M SURE SASAKI-KUN HASN'T NOTICED I'M ACTUALLY AWAKE!

NOPE ...
I'VE KNOWN THIS WHOLE TIME!
HOW COULD I NOT?!
I TRIED WAKING HER UP, BUT SHE PRETENDED NOT TO HEAR ME AND WENT BACK TO SLEEP, OR WHATEVER SHE'S DOING...
BUT WHY IS HER BLOUSE WIDE OPEN?!

I-WONDER...
IF NOBUKUNI-SAN REALLY DOES HAVE A CRUSH ON ME?
THINKING BACK, EVER SINCE I MOVED HERE...
SHE'S BEEN THROWING HERSELF AT ME PRETTY BLATANTLY.
IF IT'S TRUE, THEN AS A BOY, IT'S MY DUTY TO MAKE THE FIRST MOVE.
...?
GASP!

ぱっ
YOU CAN CATCH A SUMMER COLD NAPPING IN THE MIDDLE OF THE DAY, SO I'LL BUNDLE YOU UP WITH THIS SWEATER.
...!
?!
OO...
GRIP
PUUUUSH
......
...
PUUUUSH
WHAT IS SHE DOING?!
DOES SHE REALLY BELIEVE I'LL THINK SHE'S ASLEEP SITTING LIKE THAT?!

WHEW...

Made it work somehow.

WARU

ほわ

FUWA

ほわ

BUMP

コテッ

!

YAWN!

すー ZZZ…
すー ZZZ…
IS SHE REALLY ASLEEP?
……
HMM. MAYBE…
SHE REALLY WAS TIRED AND WASN'T COMING ONTO ME AT ALL…
キーンコーン
DIIING DOOONG
Whah !!
OH, GOSH! I PASSED OUT FOR REAL!
I'M SO SOR-RY!
…
IT'S FINE… NO SWEAT.

AWW ...
I WAS SO COMFY AROUND SASAKI-KUN THAT I DRIFTED OFF...
SQUEEZE
HE WRAPPED HIS CARDIGAN AROUND ME LIKE WE'RE CLOSE FRIENDS
THAT MAKES ME SO HAPPY...
I'LL BE SURE TO WASH IT BEFORE GIVING IT BACK...
IT'S FINE... YOU REALLY DON'T HAVE TO.

...
DID YOU SEE MY FACE WHILE I WAS ASLEEP?
...
WHAT DID YOU THINK?
UH?
WAIT, NO! I MEAN ...
DID I LOOK THAT BAD?!
SHOCK
NO... THAT'S NOT...
GULP
AAAAH! WHAT WAS WITH THAT LOUD GULP?!

I Get the
Feeling That
Nobukuni-san
Likes Me

volume
1

I Get the Feeling That Nobukuni-san Likes Me

volume 1

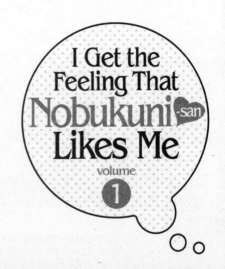

Period 3 What Boys Really Mean When They Say You're Cute!

キーンコーンカーン
DIIING DOOONG-
ガラッ
RATTLE
わやわや
CHATTER CHATTER
MORNING, NOBUKUNI-SAN...
MORN-ING!
...?
YOUR HAIR...

HUH? OH!
FUNNY STORY! I SLEPT THROUGH MY ALARM AND MY HAIR LOOKED SO BAD I JUST TIED IT BACK.
I SWEAR I'M A MORNING PERSON!
IT'S JUST THAT I GOT SO WRAPPED UP IN THE BOOK I WAS READING LAST NIGHT, I DIDN'T FALL ASLEEP UNTIL 2:00 AM...
ALSO! MY HOUSE IS, LIKE, OVER AN HOUR AWAY, SO I GOTTA WAKE UP AT 5:30 TO MAKE IT HERE ON TIME.
WHAT I MEAN IS... UH...
...
UH-HUH...
IT'S CUTE.
...!

Heh...
Hee hee ...
!
SMUSH
ぎゅむっ!!
?
STOP SMILING LIKE A GIANT DORK!
INSTEAD THINK ABOUT WHAT MEEKO-SAMA, THE LOVE GURU, TOLD YOU THIS WEEK!
PINCH
ぎー
ぎりぎりー

CHECK!
What Boys Really Mean When They Say You're Cute!

"ANY GIRL WOULD BE DANCING ON SUNSHINE AFTER A BOY CALLS HER CUTE.
"ESPE-CIALLY IF THE BOY IN QUESTION IS HER CRUSH.
YEAH!
YEAH!
JKteen
"BUT WHEN A HOT WORD LIKE 'CUTE' GETS THROWN OUT, I'M SURE THERE'RE TONS OF GIRLS WHO WORRY WHY.
YEAH!
YEAH!
YEAH!
YEAH!
"WHICH IS WHY I'M GONNA EXPLAIN TO ALL MY LITTLE LOVELORN LAMBS WHAT BOYS REALLY MEAN WHEN THEY SAY CUTE!
"THERE'RE TONS OF GUYS OUT THERE WHO DROP THE C-WORD LIKE IT'S NO BIG DEAL.
"BUT IF THEY'RE SHY OR NOT USED TO TALKING TO GIRLS, THEN WATCH OUT!"

"THOSE TYPES OF GUYS USE 'CUTE' AS A COMPLETELY INNOCUOUS WORD, DEVOID OF ANY DEEPER MEANING."
SHOOOCK!
SHY BOYS, HUH? WELL, SASAKI-KUN IS KIND OF QUIET...
WHICH IS WHY I FEEL SO COMFORT-ABLE AROUND HIM.
AS FAR AS WHETHER HE'S USED TO TALKING TO GIRLS OR NOT... I DON'T KNOW! I HAVEN'T SEEN HIM TALK TO ANY OTHER GIRL BUT ME...
SO, IT WAS PROBABLY MEANING-LESS.
HE DID ASK ABOUT MY NEW HAIRSTYLE...
I WAS RAMBLING ON FOR A LONG TIME BEFORE HE CUT ME OFF BY SAYING IT LOOKED CUTE...
OH, RIGHT! THE STUFF ABOUT MY HOUSE...

BUT WAIT... WHAT ABOUT HIM?! I DON'T KNOW ANYTHING ABOUT WHERE HE LIVES!
I DON'T CARE WHERE HIS HOUSE IS! IT COULD BE ANY-WHERE!
IT COULD BE A HOLE IN THE WALL, AND I WOULDN'T CARE! HE COULD LIVE IN A CAVE AND THAT'D BE FINE!!
NOBU-KUNI-SAN?
SASAKI-KUN...
IF YOU KNEW OF ANY GOOD CAVES, YOU'D TELL ME, RIGHT?
???
SURE, BUT I DON'T...
I'M SURE HE ONLY SAID IT TO BE POLITE...

Cute...
?!
PRICKLE...
BUT HE SAID IT THAT ONE TIME!...
Cute.
AND THAT OTHER TIME...
OH, YEAH! AND THAT TIME TOO.
ACTUALLY...
Pretty cute.
Cute.
HE'S CALLED ME CUTE A BUNCH OF TIMES!!
Only just noticed ...
NON-NON?
ARE YOU GONNA EAT?

HUH ...?
OH, GOSH! SORRY, EMA-CHAN ...
IT'S FINE. NO NEED TO APOLOGIZE.
I HAVE SOMETHING ON MY MIND, SO I'M NOT THAT HUNGRY.
DROP
NON-NON'S NOT HUNGRY ?!
RATTLE...
IT HAPPENS SOMETIMES!
RATTLE
BUT YOU'RE ALWAYS SNACKING ...
NOT ALL THE TIME!
WHEN SOMEONE SHOWS YOU THEIR BRAND-NEW GLASSES...
YOU DON'T TELL THEM THEIR OLD PAIR LOOKED BETTER!
THAT'S SUCH A SASA-CHAN THING TO SAY!
!

EITHER YOU'RE STUPIDLY HONEST OR ANNOYINGLY SERIOUS, BUT EITHER WAY... STOP GIVING BACK-HANDED COMPLIMENTS!
SERIOUSLY! PEOPLE FROM TOKYO ARE SUCH JERKS.
ALL I'M SAYING IS I THINK THE BLACK-RIMMED PAIR LOOKED BETTER ON YOUR FACE.
ズバァッ
BLUNT
YOU DON'T KNOW WHEN TO QUIT!!
LOOK, YOU CAN'T JUST GO AROUND SAYING STUFF LIKE THAT. TAKE HIS NEW RED-RIMMED GLASSES, FOR INSTANCE.
HE'S GONE WAY OUT OF HIS COMFORT ZONE BY CHOOSING TO WEAR SUCH FLASHY, EYE-CATCHING GLASSES ON SUCH A PLAIN FACE.
BUT IF WE SAID SOMETHING LIKE, "NOW THOSE ARE SOME RED GLASSES!! WHAT WERE YOU THINKING?! YOUR FACE LOOKS LIKE A WHITE CLOUD FLOATING IN A FIERY SUNSET SKY!!" HE'D BE SAD, RIGHT? SO WE KEEP IT TO OURSELVES.
YOU LITERALLY JUST SAID IT!!
YOU GUYS ARE EVEN WORSE THAN HIM!!!
ガーン
SHOCK!!
BOYS ARE SO LOUD.
ぎゃあ
RAAAH!
ぎゃあ
RRGH!
HA HA HA HA HA!
I THINK SASAKI-KUN REALLY MEANT IT WHEN HE CALLED ME CUTE...

にへっ
Hee hee!
SMUSH!!
ぎゅむうっ
UGH! YOU'RE READING TOO MUCH INTO IT!!
EVEN IF HE WAS JUST BEING POLITE, IT DOESN'T MEAN HE LIKES YOU!
THE GURU HERSELF EVEN SAID THERE COULD BE PLENTY OF OTHER REASONS TO CALL SOMEONE CUTE!
ぷる
TREMBLE
ぷる
TREMBLE
にへっ・・・・・
Hee hee
IT'S NO USE... I CAN'T STOP SMILING LIKE AN IDIOT, EVEN IF HE PROBABLY DIDN'T MEAN IT!!
NOBUKUNI-SAN? EVERYTHING OKAY?

HUH? YEAH... A-OKAY ...
HEY... SASAKI-KUN...
?
I WAS THINKING... REMEMBER HOW YOU CALLED ME... UM... CUTE BEFORE?
I MEAN, I'VE GOT A FACE LIKE A POTATO, I'M PRETTY SHORT, AND MY BODY'S THE OPPOSITE OF HOT...
WHAT I'M TRYING TO ASK IS, WHY DID YOU CALL ME CUTE?
?
WHY?
BECAUSE IT'S THE TRUTH.
"OF COURSE, SOMETIMES A GUY CALLS YOU CUTE BECAUSE HE MEANS IT."

THE NEXT MORNING.
NODOKA! IF YOU DON'T LEAVE SOON, YOU'RE GONNA MISS THE BUS!
I'M GOING RIGHT NOW!
I THINK I'M GONNA WEAR THIS HEADBAND TO SCHOOL TODAY!
"EVEN IF HE DOESN'T NECESSARILY LIKE YOU JUST YET, IT'S OBVIOUS HE THINKS YOU'RE CUTE.
"SO KEEP LOOKING CUTE, AND IT'S ONLY A MATTER OF TIME!"
I WONDER IF SASAKI-KUN WILL CALL ME CUTE AGAIN TODAY...

GOOD MORNING, NOBU-KUNI-SAN.
MORNING, SASAKI-KUN...
YOUR HEADBAND ...
FIDGET
もじっ…
IT LOOKS GOOD ON YOU. PRETTY CUTE.
Weee!!!!
TEE HEE~!

I Get the Feeling That Nobukuni-san Likes Me

volume

1

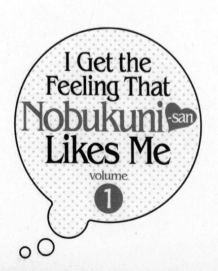

I Get the
Feeling That
Nobukuni-san
Likes Me
volume
1

Period 4   Sniffing Out the Perfect Partner?!

うろ
うろ
PACE
PACE
うろ
PACE
PACE
うろ
……

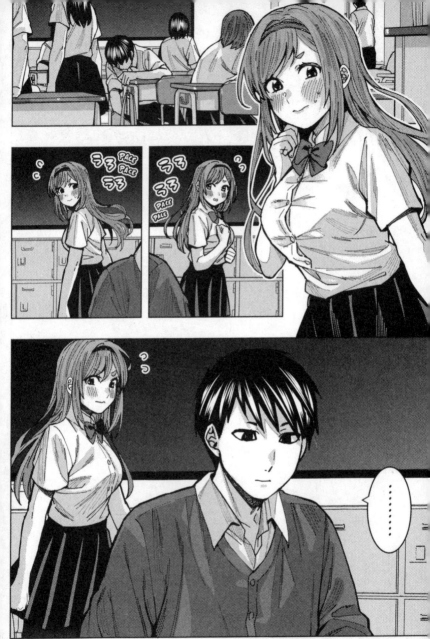

FOO!
FOO!
FOO!

?

ちらっ
PEEK

…？

すんすん
SNIFF
…

よよよ…
死ぬ

NIKUKO*! CAN I SEE YOUR NOTES FROM ENGLISH CLASS?
WHAT ARE YOU DOING?
??
UH?!! NOTHING AT ALL!!
OKAY, BUT I SAW ...
UH-UH! NOPE! YOU SAW NOTHING...!
I SWEAR I SAW YOU SECRETLY SNIFFING...
THE BACK OF SASAKI-KUN'S... EAR?

*Niku means "meat" in Japanese.
"Nikuko" is Airi's nickname for Nobukuni.

HMM?
I SWEAR I'M NOT BEING CREEPY!
TMP TMP
I CAN EX-PLAIN!
IT CAME FROM THIS WEEKLY ADVICE COLUMN!
Sniffing Out the Perfect Partner?!
CHECK!
THE LOVE GURU SAYS THERE ARE PHERO-MONES LOCATED JUST BEHIND YOUR EAR.
CHECK!
Sniffing Out the Perfect Partner?!
SO YOU SNIFF THE BACK OF YOUR CRUSH'S EAR TO SEE IF YOU'RE GENETICALLY COMPATIBLE!
I'D NEVER HEARD OF IT BEFORE, BUT EVEN LOVE IS GETTING SCIENTIFIC NOWADAYS, HUH?
OF COURSE SHE'S THE TYPE WHO WOULD TAKE A RELATION-SHIP COLUMN SERIOUSLY ...
IT'S NEWS TO ME TOO...
WHOA!
WHOA...
EVEN YOU DON'T KNOW ABOUT IT, AIRI-CHAN?!
EXCUSE ME?!
GRR!

BUT YOU'RE ALL ABOUT BOYS ...
YEAH, AND?
DO YOU REALLY BELIEVE THAT COMPATIBILITY JUNK?
IT SOUNDS PRETTY SUS TO ME.
CURIOUS
ARE YOU TRYING TO SAY MEEKO-SAMA IS A BIG PHONY?
MEEKO-SAMA?
THE LOVE GURU!
SHE'S NOT A PHONY! SHE'S THE AUTHOR OF "GIRL TALK WITH MEEKO"!
ぷぷぷ
PFFFT!
PHONY OR NOT, YOU'RE GONNA SCARE THE BOYS OFF!
I'M SURE A MAN-EATER LIKE *YOU* DOESN'T NEED HELP GETTING SOME!
WHO THE HELL ARE YOU CALLING A MAN-EATER?!
YOU DON'T EITHER, NOBUKUNI-SAN.
...!
IF YOU WANT A BOY TO LIKE YOU, DON'T RELY ON ADVICE FROM TEEN FASHION MAGAZINES.
NERVOUS
そわっ
IS IT WEIRD ...?
HUH? WELL, NO, BUT...

YOU'RE KNOWN AS A LONER, FACE ALWAYS BURIED IN A BOOK.
I HONESTLY SAW YOU AS SOMEONE WITH NO INTEREST IN BOYS OR DATING.
YEAH! SAME!
I GUESS I AM A LOSER ...
HUH? NO, NO. MORE LIKE STUDIOUS!
YOUR FAMILY'S PRETTY FAMOUS, SO YOU'RE BASICALLY LIKE A CELEBRITY.
SHE'S RIGHT! YOU'VE GOT THE BIGGEST HOUSE IN TOWN.
THANKS ...
BUT THE TRUTH IS THAT I REALLY NEED TO CHANGE WHO I AM.
HMM ...
YOU REALLY LIKE HIM THAT MUCH?
SASAKI-KUN, I MEAN.

BLUSH
~~~~~!!
SO CUTE.
CUTE...
SHE REMINDS ME OF MY DOG, SALLY...
NICE CHAT, BUT I GOTTA GO!
HUH? WHERE?
TO SMELL THE BACK OF SASAKI-KUN'S EAR...
Wasn't listening
WHOA THERE, GIRL.
WHAT'S THE PROBLEM? LUNCH WILL BE OVER SOON, AND I WANNA SNIFF HIM!
DON'T GO AROUND SAYING THAT!
YOU'RE CLEARLY A BIGGER FREAK THAN I THOUGHT.
~~~~~

HOW EXACTLY WERE YOU PLANNING ON DOING IT ANYWAY?
?
YOU WERE JUST GONNA SNEAK UP BEHIND HIM WITHOUT SAYING ANY-THING?
HUFF! HUFF!
STRAIGHT OUT OF A HORROR FILM!
BUT THERE'S NO WAY HE'LL LET ME SNIFF HIM IF I ASK...
OH, YEAH?
WANT ME TO ASK HIM INSTEAD?
HUH ?!
HEY! SASAKI-KUN!
...?
もじ
SQUIRM
もじ
SQUIRM

I HEARD ABOUT THIS NEW COMPATIBILITY TEST!
WANNA TEST IT OUT WITH ME?
UH ...?
SURE I GUESS, BUT WHY ME?
NO REASON. JUST SIT THERE.
WHAT DO YOU NEED ME TO DO?
LET ME SNIFF THE BACK OF YOUR EAR.
UM, WHAT ?!
EEEE! SHE REALLY IS A MAN-EATER ...
BUT MAYBE AFTER SHE DOES IT, I'LL BE ABLE TO ASK HIM!
DON'T MOVE, GOT IT? IT'LL HURT BIG TIME IF YOU HEAD-BUTT ME.
SURE ...

JEALOUS
はっ
GASP!
TWITCH
ぴくっ
GRRRRRR!
むむむむむむ
FUJII-SAN...
I CHANGED MY MIND.
HUH?!

WHY?
UM... WELL, 'CUZ IT'S EMBARRASSING?
HUH? I'M JUST JOKING! NOTHING TO BE EMBARRASSED ABOUT!
RIGHT? TELL HIM, NIKUKO...
DROP IT, AIRI-CHAN.
SASAKI-KUN DOESN'T WANT TO.
YOU TOO?!
THE WHOLE THING SOUNDS PRETTY WEIRD TO ME.
ARE YOU FREAKIN' KIDDING ME RIGHT NOW?!!
WHAT'S YOUR PROBLEM?!! YOU LYING DOUBLE-CROSSER!!
IF YOU DON'T DO IT TOO, I'M JUST A FREAK!

I GUARANTEE YOU WON'T BE GETTING ANY BY FOLLOWING THAT ADVICE COLUMN...
テッテレー
EMBARRASSED
WAIT A MINUTE! THAT'S MY LINE!!!
YOU'RE LIKE SOME REAL-LIFE JEKYLL AND HYDE!
WHAT THE HELL ...?
AND HERE I WAS DOING HER A FAVOR...
JUST DROP IT ALREADY.
...

AIRI...
I KNOW YOU TWO ARE CHILDHOOD FRIENDS...
SO YOU FEEL LIKE YOU HAVE TO HELP HER OUT.
BUT MAYBE YOU SHOULD CONSIDER TAKING A MORE HANDS-OFF APPROACH...
MM...
よよよ... TIP-TOE
FWIP
weet...
FINE, FINE.

I Get the Feeling That Nobukuni-san Likes Me

volume

1

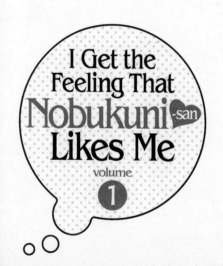

I Get the Feeling That Nobukuni-san Likes Me

volume

1

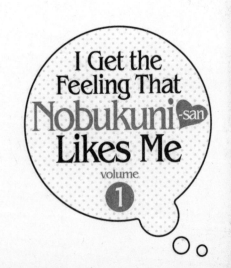

Period 5 | Ten Tips for Flirting via LINE!

CHECK!
Ten Tips for Flirting via LINE!
FLIP-WIP
FLIP
FLIP

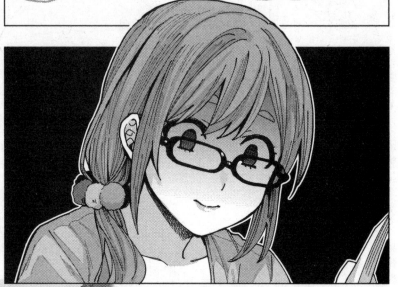

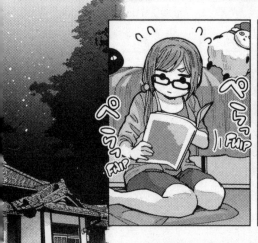

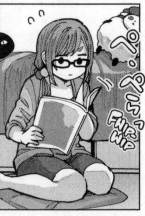

HOW TO GET A GUY USING LINE?
YEAH...
MEEKO-SAMA MENTIONED IT IN THIS WEEK'S ARTICLE.
AND YOU WANT TO TRY IT OUT ON SASAKI-KUN?
YEAH ...
LET ME GUESS... YOU DON'T KNOW WHAT HIS LINE ID IS?
YEAH ...
DO MOST PEOPLE TALK TO THEIR CRUSH ON LINE?
HUH? I DUNNO ABOUT *MOST*...

MEEKO-SAMA MENTIONED USING LINE TO GET A GUY TO FALL FOR YOU.
AND I SCOURED HER ENTIRE PIECE, BUT THERE WAS NOTHING ABOUT GETTING THE ID ITSELF.
I FEEL LIKE I'M IN A RACE WITH A BIGGER HANDICAP THAN EVERYONE ELSE...
LIKE I'M THE ONLY ONE BEGINNING FROM THE STARTING LINE...
EVERY-ONE'S GOT THEIR OWN ISSUES.
SO DO *YOU* CHAT WITH A SPECIAL SOMEONE ON LINE?
I DON'T HAVE A SPECIAL *ANYONE* RIGHT NOW.
THEN SOMEONE SPECIAL *ENOUGH?*
....
YEAH, I DO.
SEE EEEE EE?!
I TOLD *YOUUUUUU!*
GOD! YOU'RE SO FREAKIN' ***LOUD!***
AT ANY RATE, THAT'S WHY YOU CAME CRYING TO ME, HUH?
I'M NOT CRYING ...
YA KNOW, NIKUKO, IT'S NOT OFTEN HAT YOU OME TO E FOR ELP.
MY NAME'S *NOT* NIKUKO! IT'S **NODO-KA!!**

WAIT HERE AND I'LL BE RIGHT BACK.
HUH?
WHERE ARE YOU GOING ?!
HUH? TO ASK SASAKI-KUN FOR HIS LINE ID, OF COURSE.
WHAT?! YOU CAN'T DO THAT!
WHY NOT?
BE-CAUSE ...
YOU ...
YOU'RE SO MUCH CUTER THAN ME, AIRI-CHAN...
AND MY HEART WOULD BREAK IF SASAKI-KUN FELL IN LOVE WITH YOU INSTEAD.

SMUUSH
ぶにゅっ!!
ACK ?!
YOU KNOW, YOU'RE A LOT CUTER THAN YOU SEEM TO THINK.
THTO-OOOP...
ぐに
SQUISH
BE MORE CONFIDENT!
THTO-OOPPP... WET GOOO...
ぐに
SQUISH
FINE. THEN WHAT DO YOU WANT ME TO DO?
HUH? I DUNNO ...
HOW WOULD YOU DO IT?
ME? I'D JUST ASK.
MAKE A FUSS AND YOU'LL WEIRD HIM OUT.
BUT HOW DO YOU ASK?
JUST ASK!

NOT LIKE I CARE, BUT I NOTICED WE'RE NOT FRIENDS ON LINE.

WE TALK ALL THE TIME, SO I COULDA SWORN WE WERE.

WHAT'S YOUR ID SO I CAN ADD YOU?

SNUG

SASAKI-KUN...

OKAY! I'LL BE RIGHT BACK!!

SURE. YOU GOT THIS!

OKAY... WOW...

I GET IT...

LIKE THAT.

TAP TAP

...?
S-SASAKI-KUN!
LEAN
HANDS IN THE AIR!
I NOTICED YOU'RE NOT MY FRIEND!
ON LINE!
BUT WE TALK?! ALL THE TIME!!
SO I COULDA SWORN WE WERE!! FRIENDS?!
NIKUKO, A WORD?
REAL-LY?
MM-HM?! YES?!
WHY ARE YOU BEING WEIRD?
YEP!!
UH-HUH! YEP!!
YOU'RE ALWAYS SO LOUD! CALM THE HELL DOWN!

AND WHAT'S WITH THE WEIRD INFLECTIONS?
ARE YOU TRYING TO IMITATE ME?
BECAUSE I DON'T SOUND ANYTHING LIKE THAT!!
ALSO, WHAT WAS THAT WHOLE THING ABOUT PUTTING YOUR HANDS IN THE AIR? THE LINE WAS "NOT LIKE I CARE"!
STOP TRYING TO START A PARTY!
I WAS CHANNELING MY INNER AIRI-CHAN ...
BUT I'M HOPELESS...
I WAS HOPING I COULD DO IT, BUT THEN I GOT FREAKED OUT...
YOU DEFINITELY WEIRDED HIM OUT.
I DID?! *HMMM...* OH WELL.
IF YOU CAN'T ASK HIM...
THEN YOUR ONLY OTHER OPTION IS TO SOMEHOW HAVE HIM ASK YOU.
H-HOW DO WE DO THAT?
WE GOTTA GET SASAKI-KUN TO WANT TO TALK TO YOU OUTSIDE OF CLASS.
WHICH MEANS WE NEED AN INCENTIVE.

YA KNOW...

IT'S BEEN REALLY GREAT TEXTING YOU ON LINE!

SHE'S ALWAYS BEEN A GARBAGE ACTOR AND AN AWFUL LIAR...

WHAT'S SO GREAT ABOUT IT?

BEEP まご

まご BOOP

?

GOOD. HE'S LOOKING THIS WAY...

OH. YEAH?

...!

WHAT'S SO GREAT ABOUT IT?

ME! AND THE OTHERS TOLD ME TO BUTT OUT, BUT I CAN'T JUST WATCH HER DROWN!!

SHE'S FINE WHEN IT'S JUST US, SO I NEVER NOTICED HOW CLUELESS SHE REALLY IS.

EVERY MORNING YOU TELL ME WHAT COLOR PANTIES YOU'RE WEARING.
?!
WHIP
JUMP
TURN
AHH! AIRI-CHAAAN!!
WHISPER
WHY WOULD YOU SAY SOMETHING LIKE THAT OUT LOUUUD?!
ALSO, WHY WOULD ME TELLING YOU THE COLOR OF MY PANTIES BE A GOOD THING?!
CALM DOWN AND JUST FOLLOW MY LEAD.

I UNDERSTAND THE MALE MIND BETTER THAN YOU.
C C
BUT ...
YOU'LL SEE... HE'LL BE *BEGGING* TO ADD YOU IN NO TIME.
REALLY ??
....
HE'S NOT BEGGING.
HUH?! WHAT A KILLJOY.
LOOKS LIKE WE'RE MOVING TO PLAN B. WHAT COLOR PANTIES ARE YOU WEARING RIGHT NOW, NIKUKO?
WHY ?
IT'S EASIER TO GET SHY BOYS ON BOARD USING PREESTABLISHED FACTS.
BUT I DON'T REMEMBER WHAT PANTIES I PUT ON THIS MORNING ...
SQUIRM
THEN GO TO THE CORNER OF THE CLASSROOM AND CHECK.
ARE YOU FOR REAL ?!

たたたっ
TMP TMP TMP
くるっ
TURN
YOU'RE NOT JOK-ING?
たたたっ
TMP TMP TMP
......

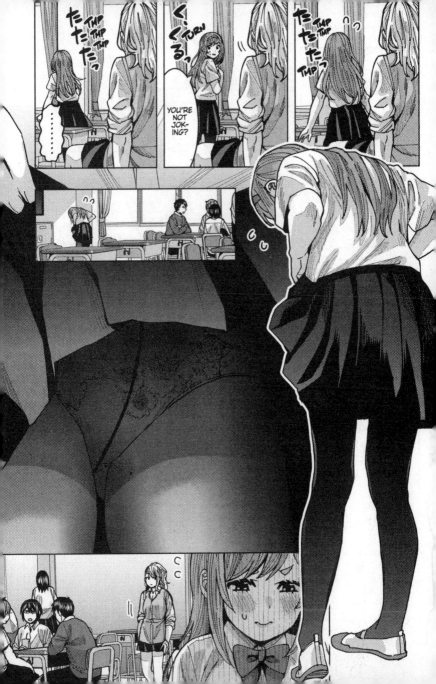

NODOKA'S PRETTY CUTE, HUH?
HUH? YEAH...
WHEN SHE COMES BACK, COULD YOU ASK HER FOR HER LINE ID?
SURE, I GUESS ...
THANKS, HON! ♥
OH! ALSO, DON'T MENTION WE HAD THIS CONVER-SATION.
THAT I TOLD YOU TO DO IT.
THEN WHAT SHOULD I SAY?
JUST ASK HER WHAT COLOR PANTIES SHE'S WEARING.
ONCE YOU'VE GONE THAT FAR, GETTING HER ID WILL BE EASY.
UM, *WHAT?*

I Get the Feeling That Nobukuni-san Likes Me

volume 1

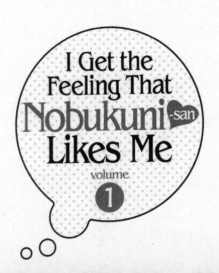

I Get the Feeling That Nobukuni-san Likes Me

volume 1

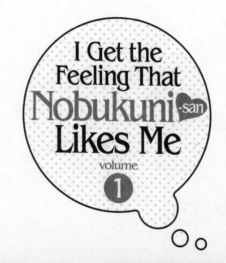

Period 6   Using Study Sessions to Make Your Move!

CHECK!

Using **Study Sessions** to Make Your **Move!**

I WANT TO SO BAD!!

I WANT TO STUDY WITH SASAKI-KUN!!

ALSO, I'VE NEVER TUTORED ANYONE BEFORE.

I'M NOT BAD AT STUDYING, AND I CAN'T OFFER TO TUTOR HIM AS HIS GRADES ARE PRETTY AVERAGE...

ORI-GAMI, HUH?

UH... ASIDE FROM ORIGAMI, I GUESS...

※ Very good at it.

CLASS
DUTY
Sasaki
Nobukuni

SMILE

...?

SQUIRM
SQUIRM

SQUIRM

SQUIRM

SQUIRM

SQUIRM

I GET THE
FEELING THAT
NOBUKUNI-SAN
REALLY WANTS
SOMETHING...

BUT WHAT?
WHAT IS IT SHE WANTS?
I'M PRETTY SURE SHE LIKES ME...
BUT SHE'S HAVING A HARD TIME SAYING SO.
IF ONLY I COULD TELL WHAT SHE WANTS... BUT I HAVE ABSOLUTELY NO CLUE...
Oh!
I SHOULD HAVE NOTICED EARLIER, NOBUKUNI-SAN...
I'VE GOT EVERYTHING HERE UNDER CONTROL...
HMM?
FEEL FREE TO GO IF YOU NEED TO.
UM... I MEAN... IT'S JUST...
YOU NEED TO GO TO THE BATHROOM, RIGHT?
SHATTER

I DON'T NEED TO GO ...
HUH?
I DON'T NEED TO GO TO THE BATH-ROOM...
YOU DON'T?!
WHY WOULD YOU THINK THAT?
TREMBLE
TREMBLE
TREMBLE
TREMBLE
SORRY! I JUST THOUGHT ...
WHY?
THAT'S NOT IT? I CLEARLY SAID THE WRONG THING...
I HAVE TO FIGURE OUT WHAT'S GOING ON BEFORE I DIG MYSELF DEEPER ...
GRRRUMBLE
!

NOBU-KUNI-SAN...
YOU'VE GOT IT ALL WRONG!
AND I'M NOT HUNGRY, EITHER!
BUT YOUR STOMACH...
WHAT-EVER NOISE YOU HEARD WAS AN UNBELIEV-ABLE COINCI-DENCE...
I STILL HAVE SOME BREAD FROM LUNCH. WANT IT?
HUH?! NO, I'M FINE!
ACTUALLY, WHAT KIND OF BREAD IS IT?
CLASS DUTY
Sasaki
Nobukuni
MEN-TAIKO* AND POTATO BREAD.
MEN-TAIKO AND POTATO BREAD...
YOU SHOULD EAT WHEN YOU'RE HUNGRY.
THANKS...

*Cod roe

I'll save this for later!
PEEK
YOU'VE ALREADY WRITTEN IN THE CLASSROOM DAILY JOURNAL, RIGHT, SASAKI-KUN?
YEAH.
IN THAT CASE, CAN YOU FINISH FILLING OUT THE REST? I'LL CLEAN THE BLACKBOARD.
HUH? SURE, I GUESS, BUT...
ASIDE FROM THE COMMENTS SECTION, WHICH WE EACH HAVE TO DO OURSELVES, SHE USUALLY TAKES CARE OF DOING THE JOURNAL...
LEAVING THE MENIAL STUFF, LIKE THE BLACKBOARD, TO ME.
BOUNCE ぷよん
BOUNCE ぷよん

ぴょん
BOUNCE
AND THIS IS WHY...
ぴょん
BOUNCE
SHE CAN'T REACH HIGH ENOUGH... SHE'S TOO SHORT...
SHE SPLIT UP THE CLASSROOM DUTIES ON PURPOSE SO IT WOULD TAKE LONGER.
Sasaki-kun also seems to be taking longer than usual, so clearly neither is in a rush to leave.

SHE'S DEFINITELY WAITING FOR ME TO DO SOMETHING BEFORE WE LEAVE.
I WISH SHE'D GIVE ME A HINT...
I ALMOST FORGOT!
...!
SASA-KI-KUN ...
...
DO YOU KNOW ABOUT CRANES?
AHH!
THIS IS DEFI-NITELY A HINT !!
I'M SURE YOU DO... AS FAR AS BIRDS GO, THEY'RE KNOWN FOR BEING A SYMBOL OF PEACE ...
LIKE THE ONE THOUSAND CRANE THING...
WOW! THAT IS A HUGE HINT!

SHE'S TRYING SO HARD, HER EARS ARE BRIGHT RED. I HAVE TO MEET HER HALFWAY!!
HEH... TEE HEE ...
A SYMBOL OF PEACE, HUH? A THOUSAND CRANES... WHAT COULD IT BE?
I HONESTLY DIDN'T REALIZE CRANES WERE SEEN AS A SYMBOL OF PEACE, BUT MAYBE IT'S NORMAL FOR THE LOCALS TO BRING THAT UP?
SPEAKING OF LOCALS, I STILL DON'T KNOW MUCH ABOUT THIS AREA.
I HAVEN'T VISITED A SINGLE TOURISTY HOT SPOT, LET ALONE THE PEACE PARK...
Aha!
I THINK I GOT IT THIS TIME!
NOBUKUNI-SAN?
ARE YOU FREE THIS WEEKEND? WELL, TOMORROW.
YEAH?
CARE TO JOIN ME FOR SOME SIGHT-SEEING?

BA-DUMP
I'D LOVE IT IF YOU COULD SHOW ME AROUND ...
HUH? WHAT?
WHY ME?
YOU DON'T WANT TO GO?
OH, YEAH... THAT'S FINE, I GUESS...
Putting it aside...
BAFFLED
OH, YEAH?! THAT'S FINE, I GUESS ?!
WHAT?! HOLD ON! I WAS SURE YOU WANTED ME TO ASK YOU OUT ON A DATE...?
THIS IS ABOUT SOMETHING ELSE.
SERI-OUSLY?! OKAY... SURE... OF COURSE...

HE'S IN SHOCK SINCE HE WASN'T EXPECTING HER TO TURN HIM DOWN.
......
OKAY, SO... I MENTIONED IT BEFORE, BUT...
I WAS HOPING I COULD TEACH YOU HOW TO DO...
!!
WAIT! DON'T TELL ME!
HUH? BUT...
I'M GONNA FIGURE IT OUT!
DO YOU WANT THE FIRST LETTER?
SURE.
OKAY... IT'S "O."
"O"?? THE WORD STARTS WITH "O," HUH?
IT'S GOT AN "O."
"O"?
"O."
O-RI-GAAAA-AAAA...?
MI!! ORIGAMI!
YOU GOT IT!

Yes!!
GRIP
Wait. What am I doing?
She had to spoon-feed me the answer.
ALSO, WHY ORI-GAMI??
......
YOU WERE TRYING TO FIGURE OUT WHAT I WANTED, RIGHT?
SORRY ...
YOU'RE REALLY SWEET, SASAKI-KUN.
......
I HAVE NO IDEA WHAT'S GOING ON.
LOOK, WHY DON'T WE WRAP THIS UP FOR NOW?
ALSO, LET ME TAKE OVER THE BLACKBOARD. YOU'LL END UP HURTING YOUR-SELF JUMPING AROUND LIKE THAT.

I like him so much♥
I like him so much!
きゅんっ♥
BA-DUMP
きゅんっ♥
BA-DUMP
S-SO, THE THING IS!
I'M ACTUALLY REALLY GOOD AT ORIGAMI, AND I WANTED TO TEACH YOU!
OH? THAT'S WHAT THIS IS ABOUT?
I CAN MAKE DRAGONS AND STUFF.
WOW!
ガーン
SERI-OUSLY?! SHOW ME HOW!
はっ
GASP!
IMMEDIATELY AFTER, SHE REALIZED SHE PICKED ORIGAMI OVER GOING ON A DATE WITH SASAKI-KUN.

I Get the
Feeling That
Nobukuni -san
Likes Me

volume
1

I Get the Feeling That Nobukuni-san Likes Me

volume 1

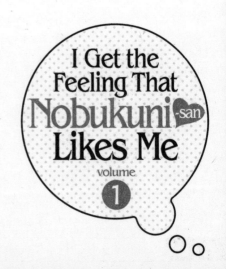

Period 7   No Boy Can Resist the Seductive Lip Bite!

CHECK!
Drive Boys Wild with the Seductive Lip Bite!
Use your front teeth to nibble on your lower lip.
That sexy look in your eye coupled with the focus on your mouth will bring out a guy's wild side.

?!!
...?
......
FINALLY LUNCH TIME!
!
TODAY'S DRAGGING MORE THAN USUAL.
MM-HM...
WHAT'S GOING ON HERE?
UH ...
SNEAK
そそくさ
NOPE ...

Let's go eat lunch!

Ema- chaaan!

· · · · · · · ·

THE MORE I THINK ABOUT IT...

THE MORE I'M CONVINCED SHE LIKES YOU.

IT'S THAT OBVIOUS?
YEP.
HMM...
WHAT ARE YOU GUYS TALKING ABOUT? WHAT'S OBVIOUS?
SHH! DON'T BE SO LOUD!
OH, YEAH! I THINK SO, TOO!
IT'S SOMETIMES PAINFULLY OBVIOUS.
YOU TWO MUST BE FLIRTING ALL THE TIME SINCE YOU SIT IN THE BACK.
THE OTHER DAY, I SAW NOBUKUNI-SAN SHOW SASA-CHAN HER ARMPITS!
WHAT?! WHY?!
※ See Period 1.

HOW DARE YOU!! YOU ONLY JUST MOVED HERE AND *ALREADY* YOU'VE STOLEN OUR NOBUKUNI-SAN AWAY FROM US!
THERE'S NO "OUR" HERE. YOU'RE THE ONLY ONE WHO'S INTO HER.
MMM...
YOU'RE NOT INTER-ESTED, SASA-CHAN?
I DIDN'T SAY THAT ...
THEN WHY NOT GO FOR IT?
SHE COMES OFF AS A PLAIN AND QUIET GIRL AT FIRST GLANCE.
BUT SHE'S ACTUALLY PRETTY CUTE.
I KNOW, RIGHT? SHE *IS* CUTE!
MM...

もぐ MUNCH MUNCH
もぐ
IF YOU MEAN "CUTE" LIKE SOME SMALL ANIMAL THEN I GUESS, BUT I STILL THINK ALL OF YOU ARE OUT OF IT.
MUNCH MUNCH もぐもぐ
もぐもぐ MUNCH MUNCH
THERE'S JUST SOMETHING ABOUT HER FACE THAT'S *CUTE.*
IT'S HARD TO PUT INTO WORDS...
WHAT'S UP?
NOTHING.
YOU LOOK LIKE YOU'RE REALLY ENJOYING THAT BREAD ROLL.
HUH? *HEE HEE*...
FROM THE WAY YOU'RE EATING, IT'S HARD TO BELIEVE THIS IS YOUR SECOND LUNCH.
WHAT'S WRONG WITH A SECOND LUNCH?!
OH, GOSH. YOU'VE GOT BREADCRUMBS ALL OVER YOUR SHIRT.
I DO?

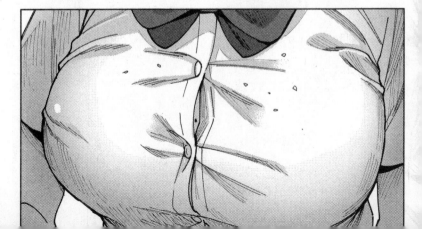

GOTTA GET RID OF 'EM.

YOU'RE RIGHT.

PAT PAT ぱた ぱた

WIPE ぱら ぱら WIPE

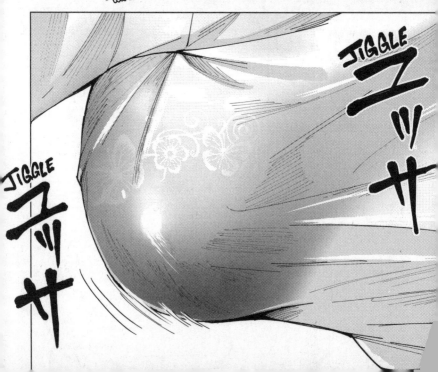

JIGGLE ヌッサ

JIGGLE ヌッサ

SHE'S PUTTING ON QUITE A SHOW.
AN AMAZING ONE.
AMAZING OR OTHERWISE...
ARE YOU SURE YOU SHOULD BE GOING AROUND OGLING OTHER GIRLS AND CALLING THEM CUTE WHEN YOU HAVE A GIRLFRIEND?
CALLING CERTAIN BODY PARTS AMAZING?
KOUSAKA-SAN IS SCARY WHEN SHE'S MAD...
Kousaka-san
HUH? SHE'S CONSTANTLY TELLING ME ABOUT ALL THE COOL GUYS IN HER AFTER-SCHOOL CLUB.
SHE DOES?
ALSO, SHE'S NOT AS SCARY AS YOU SEEM TO THINK.
SHE'S ACTUALLY REAL SWEET WHEN WE'RE ALONE.
WHAM!
STOMP すた
STOMP すた

ON THAT NOTE...
WHAT WERE WE TALKING ABOUT?
OH, RIGHT. SO WHY DON'T YOU WANT TO DATE NOBUKUNI-SAN, SASA-CHAN?
YOU'RE LITERALLY THE ONLY GUY WHO CONSTANTLY CALLS HER CUTE.
No one else does.
COME ON, SASA-CHAN. SPILL IT.
I DO THINK NOBUKUNI-SAN IS CUTE...
AND IT'S HARD FOR ME TO BELIEVE ANYONE MIGHT DISAGREE.
LOOKING AT YOU.
DON'T COME AT ME!
I WAS PREPARED TO FIGHT FOR YOU!
But it suddenly seems like everyone's against me.
ALSO, I DON'T WANT YOU GUYS TALKING ABOUT NOBUKUNI-SAN'S BREASTS.
WE'RE NOT ON HIS SIDE, EITHER.
SORRY...

SO THEN WHY DON'T YOU GO OUT WITH HER?
IS IT THAT YOU THINK SHE'S CUTE, BUT YOU DON'T *LIKE* HER?
SHE'S PRACTICALLY THROWING HERSELF AT YOU, SASA-CHAN.
YOU MUST REALLY THINK YOU'RE HOT STUFF.
HMM...
YOU GUYS REALLY THINK THAT NOBUKUNI-SAN LIKES ME?
SINCE I DON'T KNOW FOR SURE, IT SEEMS PRESUMPTUOUS TO ASSUME SHE WANTS TO GO OUT WITH ME...
WHAT?? THERE'S NO QUESTION THAT SHE LIKES YOU...
WHY WOULD WE BE TALKING ABOUT HER THIS WHOLE TIME IF WE DIDN'T BELIEVE THAT?
WE *COULD* GO BACK TO TALKING ABOUT EXACTLY HOW KOUSAKA-SAN SPOILS YOU.
L-LET'S NOT...

I MEAN!
YOU DON'T GO FLASHING YOUR ARMPIT AT JUST *ANYONE.*
BUT ...
I'VE NEVER HEARD OF FLASHING YOUR ARMPIT AT SOMEONE YOU LIKE, EITHER.
TRUE.
YOU KNOW, THINKING ABOUT THIS, FLASHING YOUR ARMPITS MAKES NO SENSE WHATSO-EVER.
MY EYES HAVE BEEN OPENED TO THE TRUTH.
IT'S CLEARLY SOME KIND OF SECRET RITUAL GIRLS DO...
SOMETHING GUYS CAN'T UNDERSTAND, LIKE SHAVING YOUR BODY HAIR...
SORRY, BUT THAT DOESN'T MAKE SENSE.
AT ANY RATE ...

IT'S NOT LIKE OUR OPINIONS REALLY MATTER, SINCE THIS IS BETWEEN THE TWO OF THEM.
キーンコーン
DHHHNG
DOOOONG
IS THAT REALLY HOW SOMEONE LOOKS AT THE PERSON THEY LIKE?
WHAT KIND OF EMOTION IS THAT ANYWAY?
SASAKI-KUN?
!

STOP STARING AT ME LIKE THAT...

YOU'RE MAKING ME SHY...

. . .

UM! ACK!

SORRY...

HURRY UP AND DATE ALREADY!!

IN THAT MOMENT, EVERYONE'S THOUGHTS ALIGNED PERFECTLY.

I Get the
Feeling That
Nobukuni -san
Likes Me

volume
1

I Get the Feeling That Nobukuni-san Likes Me

volume

1

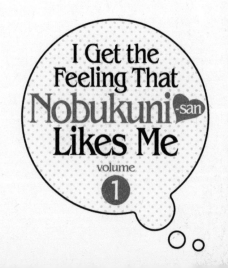

Period 8 | Give Yourself the Gift of Sexy Lingerie!

HERE, SASAKI-KUN.
HM?
SHF
I KNOW YOU HAVE A HARD TIME SEEING THE BOARD, SO HERE'S A COPY OF MY NOTES.
MY EYES HAVE BEEN GETTING WORSE LATELY.
THANKS.
YOU'RE REALLY NICE, NOBUKUNI-SAN.
HUH? IT'S NOT A BIG DEAL...
SASAKI-KUN HAS NO IDEA.

BA-DUMP
ドキドキ
BA-DUMP
ドキドキ
THAT I'M WEARING SEXY UNDER-WEAR TODAY!!

CHECK!

Give Yourself the Gift of Sexy Lingerie!

I DIDN'T HAVE ANY SEXY UNDER-WEAR, SO I SNEAKILY BOUGHT SOME OFF THE INTERNET.
THEY'RE WAY SKIMPIER THAN I WAS EXPECTING...
THE WAY THE FABRIC DIGS INTO MY BUTT IS WEIRD.
I DUNNO IF I CAN DO THIS...

NO GIVING UP, NODOKA!! YOU BOUGHT THIS LINGERIE TO BOOST YOUR CONFIDENCE, SO SIT UP STRAIGHT!
PUSH OUT THOSE BOOBIES!
PUSH
まる まる…
SLUMP SLUMP
...?
I'M SURE HE CAN SEE THEM THROUGH MY CLOTHES AND IT'S FREAKING ME OUT!

I SAT THROUGH CLASS NORMALLY, NEXT TO THE BOY I LIKE, WHILE WEARING SEXY UNDER-WEAR.
I SMILED HAPPILY WHILE HANGING OUT WITH MY FRIENDS, WHILE WEARING SEXY UNDER-WEAR.
I PASSED BY SO MANY OF MY CLASSMATES JUST LIKE ALWAYS, ACTING LIKE NOTHING WAS OUT OF THE ORDINARY, AND NO ONE HAD A CLUE...
THAT ...
I WAS ACTUALLY WEARING SEXY UNDER-WEAR.
HUFF!
HUFF!
HUFF!
HUFF!
WHY DO I FEEL SO GUILTY?!

GYM CLASS SUCKS ...
REALLY? OUR REGULAR CLASSES ARE WAY MORE BORING, SO I DON'T MIND THE BREAK.
HAVING TO CHANGE CLOTHES IS THE WORST.
I HATE HOW THE SWEAT WASHES OFF ALL MY SUN-SCREEN.
PULL
WHUH?!
WHAT'S WRONG, AIRI?
N...
NOTH-ING.

MUST BE SEEING THINGS.
I'M A-OKAY ...
I CHANGED WITHOUT ANYONE NOTICING...
?
?
I HAVE TO MAKE SURE THEY DON'T SEE...
DUN DUH-DUH-DAH
DUH-DAH
NOBU-KUNI!
STAND UP STRAIGHT!! AND PUT MORE ENERGY INTO IT!
IF I MOVE TOO MUCH ...
THE STRING HOLDING MY PANTIES UP...
WILL COME UNDONE!
SHOOF
HUH?
I SWEAR I HEARD SOME KINDA FABRIC FALL.
BOING
I CAA-AN'T!

すわっ
BLUSH
ぱっ
FWAP
A HANDKER-CHIEF?
OH, YEAH. THAT'S MINE. I MUST'VE DROPPED IT COMING OUT OF THE BATH-ROOM.

ドッ ドッ
B-DMP B-DMP
ドッ ドッ
B-DMP B-DMP
B-DMP B-DMP B-DMP B-DMP B-DMP
へなへなへな。。。
EXHAUSTED
I NEVER SHOULD'VE BOUGHT SEXY LINGERIE ...
ぐす・・・
SNIFFLE
NOT ONLY DO I FEEL WEIRD FOR WEARING THEM, BUT INSTEAD OF FEELING MORE CONFIDENT...
I'M CONSTANTLY SCARED SOMEONE WILL FIND OUT...

まるまる・・・
SLUMP SLUMP
...
NOBU-KUNI-SAN?
MM
!
YOU OKAY?
WHAT ARE YOU DOING DOWN THERE?
I'M F-FINE... EVERY-THING'S FINE.
SHF
....
じぃっ
STARE
MM
まる
SLUMP SLUMP
まるまるまる・・・
SLUMP SLUMP
DON'T LOOK AT ME!
HUH?

IT'S JUST THAT YOU LOOK...

OH! SORRY.

REALLY SEXY TODAY...

HUH ?!

Bow-Bow

HUU- UUU- UH?!

YOU LOOK REALLY SEXY TODAY AND I CAN'T HELP STARING. I'M REALLY SORRY!

I SEE...
YOU THINK I LOOK SEXY, HUH?
TEE HEE...
SASAKI-KUN'S AMAZING...
I SPENT THE ENTIRE DAY HUNCHED OVER, TRYING TO KEEP MY MOVEMENT TO A MINIMUM, AND WITH MY CONFIDENCE AT AN ALL-TIME LOW...
BUT HEARING HIM SAY SOMETHING SO SIMPLE...
MADE MY SELF-CONFIDENCE SOAR AND MY BODY FEEL LIGHTER.
たたたっ
TMP TMP TMP
くるっ
TURN
SASAKI-KUN...

SEE YA!
FLUTTER
?!
?!
NOW I GET WHAT MEEKO-SAMA MEANT ABOUT HOW WEARING SEXY LINGERIE CAN BOOST YOUR CONFI-DENCE!
MAYBE I'LL WEAR THEM TO SCHOOL AGAIN SOME-TIME.
Clueless.

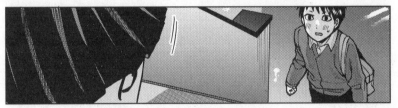

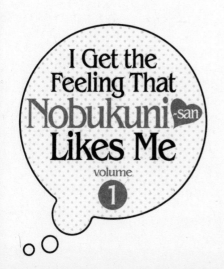

I Get the
Feeling That
Nobukuni -san
Likes Me

volume
1

I Get the Feeling That Nobukuni-san Likes Me

volume 1

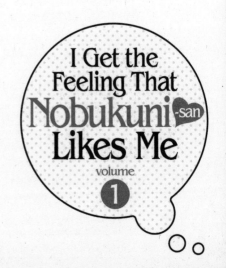

Period 9　Get Closer by Walking Home Together?! (Part 1)

OKAY, BIG GIRL!
I'M OUT.
...
HEY, BIG GIRL!
WHY ARE YOU IGNORING ME, BIG GIRL?
YOU OKAY THERE, BIG GIRL-SAN??

ぐおっ!!
RWAR
FIRST QUEEN OF LARD ASS INGDOM!
WHAT ALREADY ?!
YOU'RE SO ANNOY-ING!
AND STOP CALLING ME WEIRD THINGS IN FRONT OF SASAKI-KUN!
HUH? OH...
SORRY, MY BAD.
ME AND NODOKA GO WAY BACK.
THE TWO OF US GREW UP WAAAY OUT IN THE COUNTRYSIDE, WHICH MEANT WE HAD TO TAKE THE BUS TO SCHOOL.
THE FIRST TIME I MET HER WAS AT THE BUS STOP.

Fujii Airi, 6
Nobukuni Nodoka, 6
She was taller than Airi in elementary school!
VOUS おど
NER- おど
...
You a first year?
!
Yeah ...

Me, too!
Hi!
ふむん
ふっ
INHALE
ふむん
EXHALE
H-hi back!
The sixth-years ride with us to school, but not on the way back.
Yeah.
I practiced a lot with my mom...
もじ
FIDGET
riding the bus by myself.
もじ
FIDGET
So you can ride home with me, Airi-chan!
Sure? Okay.
I'll ride with you.
ぱあぁ
GLOOOW!
ああっ

You see! I practiced riding the bus with my mom, so it'll be okay!
LOOKING BACK, I REALIZED NODOKA WAS AFRAID OF BEING ALONE.
AT ANY RATE, FROM THAT DAY FORWARD, WE ALWAYS RODE THE BUS TOGETHER.
WE SPLIT UP AS SOON AS WE ARRIVED.
AND WE DIDN'T REALLY TALK AT SCHOOL.
BUT NO ONE ELSE LIVED CLOSE BY.
EVEN AFTER ENTERING HIGH SCHOOL, WE STILL RIDE THE BUS BACK TOGETHER. WELL, MOST OF THE TIME...
LOOK, I'M REALLY SORRY, AIRI-CHAN.

どやあっ
SMUGGG
BUT I CAN'T...
RIDE HOME WITH YOU TOMORROW.
どや
SMUG
どや
SMUG
HM? SURE, BUT...
...
OKAY.
HAVE YOU EVER BEEN TO THAT HARDWARE STORE?
YOU'RE NOT GONNA ASK ME WHY?!
I BET THEY SELL NEAT STUFF. LIKE... NAILS...
IT'S A HARDWARE STORE! OF COURSE THEY SELL NAILS AND NUTS AND BOLTS!

I CAN TELL YOU'RE BEING MEAN TO ME ON PURPOSE!
I RIDE THE BUS WITH YOU EVERY SINGLE DAY, WITHOUT FAIL, SO WHY AREN'T YOU EVEN A LITTLE BIT INTERESTED?!
ばしっ SHOVE
OUCH! OUCH! OKAY, OKAY. TELL ME, TELL ME.
ばしっ SHOVE
DOSUKOI, DOSUKOI!
STOP THAT ...

*Dosukoi *is a phrase used by sumo wrestlers during practice.*
Airi is insinuating that Nodoka is strong like a sumo wrestler.

SO? WHY CAN'T YOU RIDE HOME WITH ME?
I THOUGHT YOU WERE DONE WITH AFTER-SCHOOL DUTIES?
MY DUTIES ARE ALL DONE FOR NOW, YOU'RE RIGHT, BUT...
I TOLD SASAKI-KUN I'D WALK HOME WITH HIM TOMOR-ROW...
I FIG-URED.
DOSUKOI どすこい
YOU MOVE FAAAST!
どすこい DOSUKOI
OUCH! OUCH! I GET IT! I'VE BEEN IN YOUR SHOES BEFORE!

ARE YOU TWO GOING OUT SOMEWHERE? OR JUST STRAIGHT HOME?
HUH? JUST HOME ...
WALKING HOME TOGETHER IS A GREAT WAY TO GET TO KNOW SOMEONE BETTER...
HMM...
SASAKI-KUN'S GONNA TAKE MY PLACE...
HUH?!
NO! I...
I WON'T LET THAT HAP-PEN...

BESIDES, YOU HAD A BOYFRIEND IN JUNIOR HIGH!
AND I RODE THE BUS HOME ALONE THAT WHOLE TIME, REMEMBER?
TEE HEE! ☆
IT'LL ONLY BE FOR A SHORT WHILE, OKAY?
YOU'RE SO ANNOY-ING...
JUST DROP IT!!
YOU'VE REALLY CHANGED, BIG GIRL.
WHAT'S CHANGED? MY NAME? IT'S STILL NODOKA, NOT BIG GIRL!
NODOKA ...
YES.
NODO-KA-CHU.
NO!

HA HA HA!
UP UNTIL NOW, IT'S JUST BEEN ME TEXTING HER TO SAY I CAN'T RIDE THE BUS BACK WITH HER 'CAUSE I'VE GOT PLANS...
THINKING ABOUT IT, I DON'T THINK SHE'S EVER CANCELED ON ME.
ALSO...
HEY...
THAT LOVE GURU YOU LIKE SO MUCH...
MEEKO-SAMA? THE LOVELORN LAMB HERDER?
THAT'S HER.
SINCE WHEN DID YOU GET SO INTO HER?
AROUND JUNIOR HIGH.
I...

I WAS BORN A SMALL-TOWN GIRL...
BUT I DIDN'T GO INTO TOWN ALL THE TIME LIKE YOU DID, AIRI-CHAN.
I STAYED AT HOME, WITH MY BOOKS.
AND I REALIZED I WAS GOING TO START HIGH SCHOOL WITHOUT KNOWING ANYTHING...
I FIGURED IF I TRIED TO ACT MORE LIKE A NORMAL HIGH SCHOOL GIRL...
LIKE READING DATING COLUMNS IN TEEN FASHION MAGAZINES ...
THEN MAYBE I'D *BECOME* A NORMAL TEENAGE GIRL.
OF COURSE SHE TURNED TO A BOOK FOR HELP.
I KNEW I'D HAVE TO CHANGE SO SASAKI-KUN WOULD NOTICE ME...
FOR A WHILE IT WAS LIKE I COULDN'T RIDE THE BUS WITHOUT HER STICKING TO ME LIKE GLUE, IMITATING EVERYTHING ABOUT ME.
BUT EVER SINCE FINDING THIS NEW ROLE MODEL, SHE'S CHANGED.
I ALWAYS CONSIDERED HER MY BEST FRIEND IN JUNIOR HIGH SCHOOL...
BUT EVER SINCE WE GRADUATED, WE STOPPED HANGING OUT.
IS THIS WHERE WE PART WAYS?

I GUESS THAT'S JUST PART OF GROWING UP...
SO DID THAT WHATEVER-HER-NAME-IS LOVE GURU ...
DO A COLUMN ABOUT GETTING TO KNOW SOMEONE BY WALKING HOME TOGETHER?
HUH ...?
NO, SHE DIDN'T.
BUT THAT'S HOW I BECAME BEST FRIENDS WITH *YOU*, AIRI-CHAN.
RIGHT?

?
YOU REALLY HAVE CHANGED, NODOKA.
HUH? WHY DO YOU SAY THAT?
PERSONALLY, I LIKE YOU THE WAY YOU ARE.
DON'T FEEL PRESSURED TO LOSE WEIGHT.
THERE'S NO ONE PRESSURING ME TO LOSE WEIGHT!

Period 10 Get Closer by Walking Home Together?! (Part 2)

DIIING DOOONG
カーン
コーン

DIIING DOOONG
キーン
コーン

WELL THEN...

UM...

LET'S GO?

SURE.

TODAY'S THE DAY I TOLD SASAKI-KUN I'D WALK HOME WITH HIM.

HEH... TEE HEE...

PEEK
WHAT'S UP?
NOTH-ING!
EVERY-THING'S FINE!
...
THE BUS I NEED TO TAKE ACTUALLY LEAVES FROM THAT STATION OVER THERE...
BUT I LIED SO WE COULD SPEND TIME TOGETHER.
TMP TMP
I'LL JUST WAIT FOR THE PERFECT MOMENT TO SNEAK AWAY AND HEAD BACK.
MORE IMPORTANTLY, THIS IS MY CHANCE FOR SOME ONE-ON-ONE TIME WITH HIM OUTSIDE OF SCHOOL!
I GOTTA MAKE MY MOVE!

FUZZY
WARM
HAPPY
HAPPY
FREEZE
THIS IS NO TIME TO BASK IN THE GLOW OF HAPPI-NESS!
BEING ALONE WITH SASAKI-KUN MADE ME SO HAPPY, I LOST TRACK OF TIME!
I NEED TO START HEADING BACK!
NOBU-KUNI-SAN?
...!
WHAT'S UP?

I WAS JUST WONDERING WHICH WAY YOU GO TO GET HOME.
HUH?
WHAT?! WE'VE ALREADY WALKED THIS FAR?
I REALLY NEED TO START HEADING BACK, BUT I STILL HAVEN'T DONE ANYTHING YET, AND I WANT MORE TIME WITH HIM...
HMPH!
WHICH WAY DO YOU GO, SASAKI-KUN?
HUH? ME?
THIS...
WAY.
WAY !!
MY HOUSE IS THIS WAY, TOO!!

LOOKS LIKE IT...

I GUESS WE'RE GOING THE SAME WAY...

WE CAN WALK TOGETHER A LITTLE LONGER...

YOU KNOW, GROWING UP IN TOKYO...

YEAH?

WHY?

I ALWAYS WANTED TO LIVE IN A SMALL TOWN.

LIVING IN A BEAUTIFUL PLACE LIKE THIS...

WALKING TO AND FROM SCHOOL ALONG THE COASTLINE...

HA HA HA ...

I'M SURE YOU'RE USED TO IT BY NOW, GROWING UP HERE.

OH GOD! WHERE EVEN ARE WE RIGHT NOW?!!
I'M COM-PLETELY LOST.
I'M SURE NONE OF THIS FEELS THAT SPECIAL TO YOU, HUH?
WHERE THE HELL ARE WE?!!
AND I GUESS ...
FWOOSH
I'VE GOTTEN USED TO IT AS WELL.

I LOST THAT SPARK OF EXCITE-MENT...
SASAKI-KUN.
MOVING HERE FROM TOKYO MUST HAVE BEEN TOUGH.
I'M SURE THERE WAS A LOT YOU HAD TO GET USED TO.
ALSO, I'M SURE YOU HAD FRIENDS YOU LEFT BEHIND... MAYBE EVEN A SPECIAL SOMEONE...
BUT FOR ME...
YOU BECAME PART OF MY EVERYDAY LIFE...
AND THAT MAKES ME...
HAPPY...
NOBU-KUNI-SAN...
TEE HEE...

SEE YOU TOMORROW!

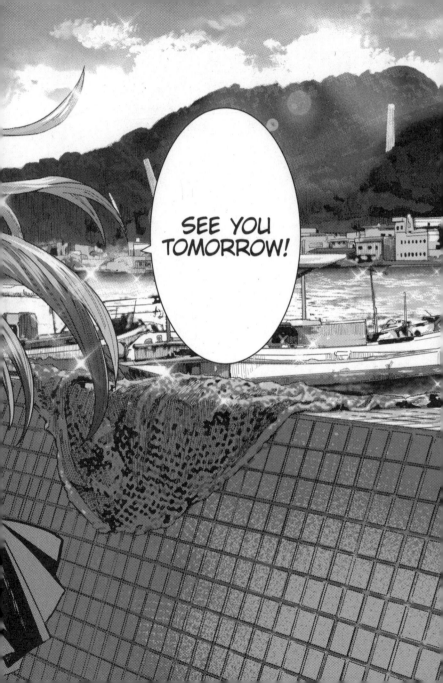

YEP.

SEE YOU TOMOR- ROW!

GHOOF

PEEK

I'LL JUST WAIT HERE FOR A MOMENT BEFORE TURNING BACK...
LET'S SEE... TRAIN TIMES...
WAIT, I NEED TO LOOK UP BUS TIMES, TOO.
?
IT'S GONNA TAKE ME ABOUT THIRTY MINUTES TO WALK BACK TO SCHOOL...
AND I STILL DON'T KNOW WHERE I AM!!
I GUESS...
I'M GOING HOME ALONE, HUH?

WHAT ARE YOU DOING HERE, SASAKI-KUN?
ISN'T YOUR HOUSE IN THAT DIRECTION?
ISN'T YOURS TOO?
...
AH.
WELL THEN... UM...
LET'S WALK TOGETHER?
SURE...
TEE HEE...
To be continued in Volume 2.

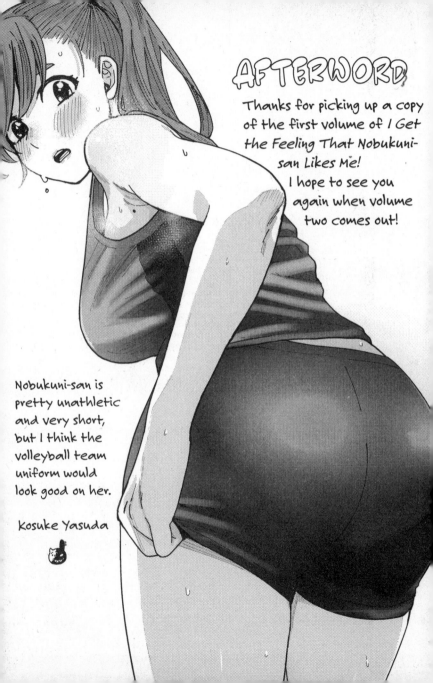

AFTERWORD

Thanks for picking up a copy of the first volume of *I Get the Feeling That Nobukuni-san Likes Me!* I hope to see you again when volume two comes out!

Nobukuni-san is pretty unathletic and very short, but I think the volleyball team uniform would look good on her.

Kosuke Yasuda

SEVEN SEAS ENTERTAINMENT PRESENTS

I Get the Feeling That
Nobukuni-san Likes Me

story and art by KOSUKE YASUDA

VOLUME 1

TRANSLATION
Miki Z

ADAPTATION
Asha Bardon

LETTERING
Robert Harkins

LOGO DESIGN
George Panella

COVER DESIGN
Nicky Lim

PROOFREADER
Tori Bowler

COPY EDITOR
B. Lillian Martin

EDITOR
McKenzie Carnahan

PRODUCTION DESIGNER
Christa Miesner

PRODUCTION MANAGER
Lissa Pattillo

PREPRESS TECHNICIAN
Melanie Ujimori
Jules Valera

EDITOR-IN-CHIEF
Julie Davis

ASSOCIATE PUBLISHER
Adam Arnold

PUBLISHER
Jason DeAngelis

TONARI NO NOBUKUNI-SAN WA ORE NO KOTO GA SUKI NA KIGASURU
by KOSUKE YASUDA
© Kosuke Yasuda 2021
All rights reserved.
First published in Japan in 2021 by HAKUSENSHA, INC., Tokyo.
English language translation rights arranged with HAKUSENSHA, INC., Tokyo
through TOHAN CORPORATION, Tokyo.

Seven Seas press and purchase enquiries can be sent to Marketing Manager Lianne
Sentar at press@gomanga.com. Information regarding the distribution and purchase of
digital editions is available from Digital Manager CK Russell at digital@gomanga.com.

Seven Seas and the Seven Seas logo are trademarks of
Seven Seas Entertainment. All rights reserved.

ISBN: 978-1-63858-555-8
Printed in Canada
First Printing: November 2022
10 9 8 7 6 5 4 3 2 1

READING DIRECTIONS

This book reads from *right to left*,
Japanese style. If this is your first time
reading manga, you start reading from
the top right panel on each page and
take it from there. If you get lost, just
follow the numbered diagram here.
It may seem backwards at first,
but you'll get the hang of it! Have fun!!

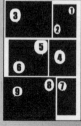

Follow us online: www.SevenSeasEntertainment.com